Video Talks for Kids

50 Bible Messages Using Video Clips

by Patricia Alderdice Senseman

™

STANDARD
PUBLISHING

Cincinnati, Ohio

Dedication

To the children of Southeast Christian Church, Christ's Church at Mason, and River Hills Christian Church who helped me appreciate the value of using videos to get their attention.

Video Talks for Kids

© 2000 Standard Publishing

Published by Standard Publishing, Cincinnati, Ohio
A division of Standex International Corporation

Credits

Cover design by Jeff Jansen
Interior design by Mike McKee
Acquisitions editor: Ruth Frederick
Editor: Dale Reeves

07	06	05	04	03	02	01	00
5	4	3	2				

ISBN: 0-7847-1161-5
Printed in the United States of America

Contents

How to Use This Book

Kids Love Movies

Children go to the movie theaters to watch movies. They rent movies at the video store. They borrow movies from the library. They exchange videos with their friends. They watch movie channels on cable television. They watch reruns of movies on the major and minor TV networks.

And moviemakers love kids. Every year more and more children's blockbusters are released into the marketplace. New production companies that are targeting children are being incorporated all the time.

In a new century full of media awareness, what better way to reach kids where they are than to use movies? By showing a clip from a popular movie, you immediately grab the children's attention. You meet them where they are. You begin with something that is familiar to them and lead them to discover a biblical principle.

Roll 'Em

As you start using movie clips to grab your children's attention, you will want to follow these simple guidelines:

◆ Always preview the clip you are going to use. You will be able to more finely tune the point that you want to make by watching the clip ahead of time. And you won't be embarrassed by ignorance! Standard Publishing does not necessarily endorse the entire content of each movie.

◆ Set up the clip before you show it and follow up the clip after you show it. You may want to summarize what has taken place in the movie so far before you show a clip. You may want to review the events in a movie clip right after showing it. Have several introductory and summary statements prepared.

◆ Some of the movie clips you may want to rewind and show twice. The action or dialogue may go so quickly that the children may need to hear it twice. Show the clip once. Then tell the children what to listen for the second time.

A Word About the Copyright Law

The United States Copyright Act treats displays or performance of multimedia presentations, films, and videotapes by nonprofit organizations (including churches) to a small group of individuals as "public performances" even if no admission fee is charged. The fact that the church or one of its members may have purchased the copy of the film or videotape makes no difference. To avoid breaching the "public performance" prohibition in the Copyright Act, you must in each instance secure the copyright owner's permission or alternatively obtain an "umbrella license" from the Motion Picture Licensing Corporation. To learn more about the umbrella license, contact the MPLC at 1-800-462-8855 or visit them on the web at www.mplc.com.

Your church can apply for a blanket licensing agreement for about $100 a year. You may also want to visit http://fairuse.stanford.edu/ for additional information on the Copyright Act and the "Fair Use Doctrine."

A Message from Your Sponsor

Each video clip used in this book includes the following:

Topic–Each clip centers around at least one topic relevant to children's issues. The clips are presented in alphabetical order according to topic. An alphabetical index of movie titles is included at the end of the book.

Activity idea–The topic of the movie clip is developed using an interactive activity, teacher talk, and discussion questions. Adapt what is provided to make them applicable to your group.

Start and stop times–The VCR counter numbers are given for the beginning and end of each clip. Rewind the video, set the counter to 00:00, and fast-forward to the clip. Verbal and action cues are also provided for each clip.

Clip summary–Basic information is provided to summarize the movie action. Use this information to set up the clip.

Related Scripture–Scripture passages appropriate for elementary-aged children are listed and indexed to aid you in using this book. Flip to the index at the back of the book to find a clip that correlates with a particular lesson. The movie clip will help you connect with your students, but the power for change in their lives comes from the living and active Word of God!

Where to Find Them

Videos are everywhere! Check with families in your church, advertise in your church newsletter, visit public libraries, video stores, and groceries.

If you cannot find a video available for rent or purchase via these outlets, you may want to search these e-stores by browsing for videos at:

- www.family.org/resources (or call 800-232-6459)
- www.christianbook.com
- www.ichristian.com
- www.guidinglightvideo.com
- www.crownvideo.com

Start time 14:03

Start cue

Narrator: "The morning of the terrible crime started like any other . . ."

End time 15:84

End cue

The duck says, "I'm aller-gic to cats; they make me sneeze."

Clip summary

A duck has decided to crow like a rooster each morning so that he won't be eaten by the farmer and his wife. This is successful until the farmer's wife buys an alarm clock to wake them up each morning. The duck plots with Babe to steal the alarm clock.

Materials

Cued video, TV, VCR, stuffed farm animals such as a duck, pig, cat, dog, sheep, rooster, hen, horse, and cow

Say

"God created many, many animals. There are so many different animals we cannot even name all of them. Let's see how many we *can* name."

Guide students to name as many animals as they can. Suggest categories as they name animals to stimulate their thinking. Some examples include farm animals, zoo animals, jungle animals, water animals, animals in our homes, and animals that fly.

Ask students

◆ Have you seen the movie *Babe*?

◆ What kind of animal is Babe?
◆ Where does Babe live?
◆ What are some of the other farm animals in the movie?

Before the clip, say

"Farmer Hoggett's wife just bought an alarm clock to help her and her husband wake up in the mornings. A duck on the farm has been trying to crow like a rooster so that he won't be killed and eaten for dinner. He thinks the rooster has an important job. The duck thinks if he has an important job then he won't be killed. He is very upset about this alarm clock that could replace him. Let's watch to see what happens."

Show the video clip.

Say

"God created every animal with a purpose—even a skunk! The duck's purpose was not to crow like a rooster. That was the rooster's purpose."

After viewing the clip, give each child a stuffed animal.

Ask students

◆ What is the purpose of the animal you have?
◆ What did God create that animal to do?

Help students see the unique purpose of each animal: cats catch mice, roosters crow at dawn, hens lay eggs, horses work on the farm, cows give milk, and so on.

Say

"God also created every human being for a special purpose! Each one of us has special abilities that we can use to make our world better. Some of us sing. Some of us are funny. Some of us talk very well. Some of us like to work hard. Every single one of us is important. When we all work together, using our individual abilities, the world is a much better place. So don't be a duck acting like a rooster!"

Related Scripture

Exodus 31:1-5
1 Corinthians 12:14-20
Ephesians 4:11-13
1 Peter 4:10, 11

Start time 8:70

Start cue

The announcer says, "With the Angels down by seven . . ."

End time 11:62

End cue

The manager turns over a table of food in the locker room.

Clip summary

The Angels' outfielders fumble a catch. The Angels' manager and the pitcher are angry and start fistfighting one another, clearing the Angels' bench.

Materials

Cued video, TV, VCR

Ask students

◆ Have you ever been in a fistfight?
◆ What started it?

Before the clip, say

"When people fight, it's usually because they are angry. Sometimes ball players get angry when the game is not going their way. They may be losing, or their team may not be playing well. In the movie *Angels in the Outfield*, the Angels' manager gets very mad when his team is not winning a game. Let's watch to see what he does."

 Show the video clip.

Ask students

◆ What does it mean to be angry?
◆ When have you been angry?

Encourage students to think of specific times when they were angry. Have several of the children tell about being angry. Prompt them with questions as necessary.

Ask students

◆ What happens when you are angry?
◆ How do you feel when you are angry?

Help the children understand that they need to think carefully when they are angry. It's easy to get caught up in the moment and say or do something that they will later regret. Guide the children to give examples of a time when this happened to them.

Say

"The Bible tells us to be careful when we are angry. We must not sin when we are angry."

Ask students

◆ How can we be angry and not sin?
◆ How can we appropriately express our anger?
◆ How should we *not* express our anger?

Discuss with the children that there are appropriate and inappropriate ways to express anger. You may want to role-play situations when a child is angry and what to do that is appropriate and what is inappropriate.

Related Scripture

Genesis 4:3-8
Proverbs 29:11, 22
Matthew 5:21-24
Ephesians 4:26, 27

Start time 20:38

Start cue

Jenny Gourd asks, "Have you ever seen a boy with funny clothes?"

End time 21:19

End cue

The end of the song.

Clip summary

The VeggieTale characters sing, "I Can Be Your Friend"—a song that emphasizes the differences of people. God makes people in all different shapes, colors, and sizes with varying gifts, talents, and abilities. Even though everyone is different, we can all be friends.

Materials

Cued video, TV, VCR, poster board, markers

Create a poster with the children's names listed down the left side. Across the top, list the following: hair color, eye color, height, number of siblings, what you had for breakfast, and month of your birthday. Leave room for one more column but do not label it.

Say

"God made each of us unique. There is no one else exactly like you."

Ask students

◆ What are some ways in which we are all the same?
◆ What are some ways in which we are different from each other?

Say

"Look at this chart. Do you think that anyone else will fill in all of the blanks exactly like you do?"

Have the children fill in the blanks on the chart. When all of the children have finished, point out the similarities and the differences on the chart. Some children will have the same hair and eye color. Some children will have the same number of siblings. But no one will be exactly the same.

Before the clip, say

"Even though we are different from each other, we still have fun together. We can be friends."

 ## Show the video clip.

Say

"The VeggieTale characters learned that they could be friends even though they were different from each other and had different abilities. Think about what abilities you have."

Ask students

◆ What are you talented at doing?
◆ What is a special gift that you have?

Guide the children to list their ability, talent, or gift in the last column.

Say

"God made you in a unique way for a very special purpose."

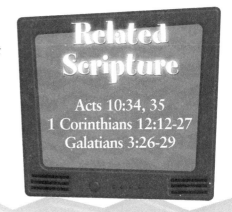

Related Scripture

Acts 10:34, 35
1 Corinthians 12:12-27
Galatians 3:26-29

Start time 30:44

Start cue
Scott Calvin (Tim Allen) says, "S.C.?"

End time 34:50

End cue
Charlie asks, "Have you ever seen a million dollars? Just because you haven't . . ."

Clip summary
Charlie is trying to convince people that his dad is Santa Claus and that they rode a sleigh to the North Pole. No one will believe his farfetched tale.

Materials
Cued video, TV, VCR, Bible

Ask students
◆ Have you ever known something was true but no one else would believe you?

Encourage children who respond to share their stories.

Before the clip, say
"In the movie *The Santa Clause*, Charlie was with his dad on Christmas Eve when his father turned into Santa Claus. They had to deliver presents and return to the North Pole. Charlie knew his dad was Santa Claus because he saw it happen with his own eyes. He was with Santa, his dad, in Santa's workshop. When Charlie tells people what happened, no one will believe him—not his mom or stepfather, his friends, or his teacher. But Charlie knows it is true."

Show the video clip.

Ask students

◆ Why was Charlie so sure his dad was Santa Claus?
◆ How do you know that Jesus is God's Son?
◆ How do you know that he was born in a manger and died on a cross for our sins?

Say

"Charlie asked Neil, his stepfather, 'Have you ever seen a million dollars? Just because you haven't seen it doesn't mean it doesn't exist.' We haven't seen Jesus in the flesh, have we? Does that mean he doesn't exist?"

Ask students

◆ How do we know that Jesus existed?

Say

"We need to have faith that Jesus is God's Son. We have to believe in something that we cannot see."

Read Hebrews 11:1, 6. These verses say that faith is being sure of what we do not see. By our faith we please God. You may want to distinguish here between fantasy (Santa Claus) and the real thing (Jesus).

Ask students

◆ Just because we cannot see our birthdays, does that mean we do not have them?
◆ Does that mean they are not coming this year?

Say

"Charlie believed that his dad was Santa Claus because he had seen evidence that proved he was Santa. We can't see Jesus, but we can have faith that he is who he says he is."

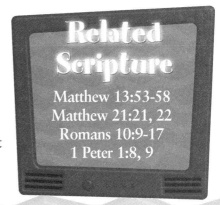

Related Scripture

Matthew 13:53-58
Matthew 21:21, 22
Romans 10:9-17
1 Peter 1:8, 9

Start time 10:18

Start cue

Winnie says, "I just found him like this."

End time 11:29

End cue

Silas says, "That dog is my property and I'm going to call the sheriff . . . you hear?"

Clip summary

The Last Chance Detective kids rescue a man's dog because it is sick and the owner will not take him to a vet for treatment. They take the dog off the man's property without his permission.

Materials

Cued video, TV, VCR

Ask students

◆ When is it difficult to make the right choice?
◆ Have you ever done the wrong thing yet felt it was the right thing to do? Explain.

Ask the children to recall several examples of when doing the wrong thing made some sense to them. You may want to give a couple of examples to get them started.

Before the clip, say

"The kids in this video clip make a decision. Watch the clip and decide if what they do is right or wrong."

 Show the video clip.

Ask students

◆ Was it right or wrong for the kids to take the man's dog?
◆ The kids wanted to help the dog. Did that make it right to take it to the vet?
◆ The dog belonged to the man. Were they stealing by taking him?

Guide the conversation to discuss the two sides of this issue: the dog was the man's property and the kids should not have taken it; that is stealing. The man was neglecting the dog's care; if he had a dog, he should take care of it.

Ask students

◆ What would you have done?
◆ Should the kids have returned the dog back to the man, knowing that he would not take care of it?
◆ What would have been appropriate for the kids to do?

Lead the children to see that the Last Chance Detective kids could have offered to pay for the dog's care at the vet. Or they could have talked to the vet or a parent about the dog.

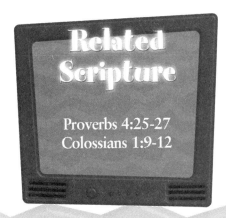

Related Scripture

Proverbs 4:25-27
Colossians 1:9-12

The Not-So-Great Escape

McGee and Me series

Start time 15:61

Start cue

Sounds are coming from the movie screen, while the kids are wearing 3-D glasses.

End time 18:38

End cue

Dad says, "I'll be up in a little while to talk about your punishment."

Clip summary

Nicholas wants to see a scary movie with a friend but his parents said no. He decides to sneak out of the house to see it without his parents' knowledge. This clip is a song emphasizing that what we put into our minds is often lived out in our lives.

Materials

Cued video, TV, VCR

Ask students

◆ Why is it difficult to make good choices sometimes?
◆ Is there always one right choice?

Guide children to discuss how difficult it is to be decisive and to choose what is right and wrong when there is a gray area or when there may be more than one choice.

Say

"In this video clip, Nicholas wants to go to a scary movie with his friend. His parents told him he could not go because the content of the movie is not something he should put into his mind."

Ask students

◆ What do you think Nicholas should do?
◆ What would you do?

Discuss the pressure Nicholas must feel. He wants to see the movie because other kids at school will. His friend may pressure him to go with him anyway.

Say

"Nicholas decides he is going to go anyway. He sneaks out of the house and meets his friend."

Ask students

◆ What do you think will happen because Nicholas makes this choice?
◆ What would happen to you?

Before the clip, say

"Let's watch to see what happens next."

 Show the video clip.

Ask students

◆ Did Nicholas have a good time at the movie? What makes you think that?
◆ Did Nicholas like the movie? What makes you think that?
◆ What was the reaction of Nicholas' parents? Why were they disappointed?

Help the children to see that Nicholas disappointed his parents by disobeying, he was punished, he didn't have a good time, or even enjoy the movie.

Related Scripture

Proverbs 3:1-8
Jonah 1:1-17
Ephesians 6:1-3

Start time 17:45

Start cue

Charlie Brown says, "I guess I really don't know what Christmas is all about."

End time 18:30

End cue

Linus says, "That's what Christmas is all about, Charlie Brown."

Clip summary

Charlie Brown is searching for the true meaning of Christmas. Linus sets him straight by reciting the story of Jesus' birth from Luke 2.

Materials

Cued video, TV, VCR, Bible, supplies for communion

Ask students

◆ What do you love about Christmas?
◆ What is one of your favorite things to do during the Christmas season?
◆ Why is it so easy to spend all your time thinking about "getting" at Christmas?

Before the clip, say

"There is a famous person who wanted to understand more about Christmas, but he was having trouble finding answers to his questions. I'm talking about Charlie Brown. Charlie wanted to know more about what is really important at Christmastime. As he watched and talked to his friends, he observed that they seemed to be greedy. (*Ask a child to define what it means to be greedy*.) He knew that isn't what Christmas is about. So Charlie Brown talked to Linus. Linus could always set him straight."

 ## Show the video clip.

Ask students
◆ What did Charlie Brown discover Christmas is all about?
◆ How can knowing the true meaning of Christmas change your life?

Say
"We know what Christmas is really all about. It's about God loving the world so much that he sent Jesus to die for everyone."

Read John 3:16 together or have one child read it.

Say
"God loved us so much that he was willing to sacrifice his very own Son so that we could live. That's what Christmas is all about. And that's what communion is all about: remembering what Jesus did for us when he died on the cross for our sins."

Pray, thanking God for the gift of his Son at Christmas and the sacrifice of Jesus at Easter. Then take communion together.

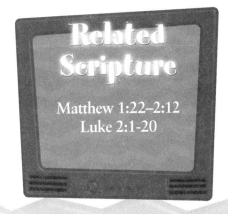

Related Scripture

Matthew 1:22–2:12
Luke 2:1-20

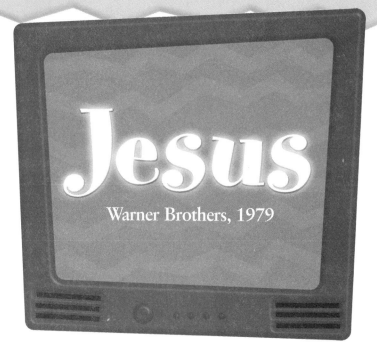

Warner Brothers, 1979

Start time 00:68

Start cue

Narrator: "For God so loved the world . . ."

End time 04:15

End cue

Narrator: "The shepherds hurried to see the newborn babe in the manger . . ."

Clip summary

An angel appears to Mary announcing that she is to give birth to the Messiah. She visits her cousin Elizabeth. Jesus is born in Bethlehem. The shepherds hear of the birth and visit the manger.

Materials

Cued video, TV, VCR

 Show the video clip.

Discuss the meaning of John 3:16 at Christmas. Then choose one of these games to play with the events portrayed in the video.

Birth Order Race

Have the children race to place the events in chronological order. You could give them slips of paper with one event on each slip of paper. Or simply tell them how many events are portrayed in the video. The children could play individually, in pairs, or in teams.

Clue by Clue

Give clues for one of the events from the video until the children guess it. Start with a difficult clue and get progressively easier until a child guesses the event. Depending upon the children's ages and skill level, they could guess individually or as teams.

What's the Object?

Give the children an object that relates to each event in the video. Have the children match the object to the event. Then place the objects in chronological order with the events. The objects could be simple for younger children and more difficult for older children.

Follow the game time with a discussion about Jesus' birth.

Ask students

◆ How was Jesus' name chosen?
◆ Who was Elizabeth's baby?
◆ Why were Mary and Joseph in Bethlehem?
◆ How did the shepherds find out about Jesus' birth?
◆ Why did Jesus come to earth?
◆ Who first told about Jesus' birth?

Related Scripture

Luke 1:5-38
John 1:1-18

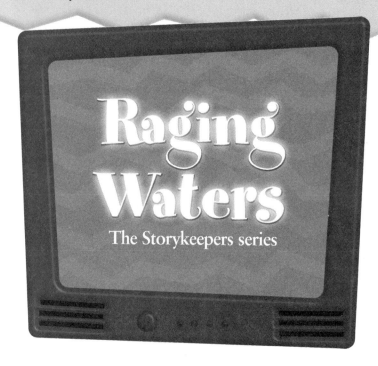

Start time 9:49

Start cue

The guard says, "Hail Caesar."

End time 11:70

End cue

Nero says, "He shall be an example to all of Rome on how we deal with Christians."

Clip summary

Zak, a Christian boy living in the first century, is taken before Nero because he is found with a scroll telling about one of Jesus' miracles. Nero is the Roman ruler who martyred hundreds of Christians because they believed in Jesus. Nero decides to feed Zak to the lions because of his faith.

Materials

Cued video, TV, VCR

Ask students

◆ If someone asked you to explain why you believe in God, what would you say?
◆ If someone said, "How can you believe in something you can't see?", what would you say?

Before the clip, say

"The first century was almost 2000 years ago. It was right after Jesus had returned to Heaven. During the first century there was a Roman ruler named Nero who persecuted the Christians. He even killed people because they were Christians, but the Christians didn't stop believing in God. They just had to hide. They got together and worshiped in secret. One of the things they did when they gathered together was retell the stories of Jesus—stories of his miracles, of his teachings, how he died and came back to life. Let's watch part of a video that shows when a young boy is caught smuggling a scroll with a story about Jesus written on it. He is taken before Nero."

 ## Show the video clip.

Ask students

◆ How do you think Zak felt when he was standing before Nero?
◆ What would you say if someone said to you, "I don't understand why people insist on throwing away their lives for some dead Jewish carpenter"?
◆ What would be hard about believing in Jesus if you were Zak?

Have the children act out the video clip. Assign the parts of the guards, Zak, and Nero to various children. Challenge the child playing Zak to be brave and stand up to Nero. Give several sets of children opportunities to act out the scene.

Next, describe a modern-day situation in which children are faced with defending their faith. For example, it might be defending creation when a teacher is discussing evolution. It could be talking to a child on the playground who is Jewish, Hindu, or an atheist. Choose a situation that is appropriate for your group. Assign parts and have the children rehearse what their responses might be.

Ask students

◆ Why are Jesus' miracles great to tell people who do not believe in Jesus?

Say

"Jesus performed miracles so that we would believe that he is the Son of God. When we defend our faith, that's what we want other people to believe as well."

Related Scripture

Daniel 6:1-27
John 20:24-31
1 Peter 1:3-12
1 Peter 4:12-14

Start time 44:50

Start cue

Mary says, "Do you think we'll ever get finished, Dickon?"

End time 45:60

End cue

Mary says, "You just planted your first rose."

Clip summary

Mary and Dickon are working in the secret garden. They've taken Colin with them for the first time. The kids show the garden to the gardener. He calls Colin "crippled" and "dim-witted" because he has a disability. Mary and Dickon demonstrate how Colin can help in the garden in spite of his disability.

Materials

Cued video, TV, VCR

Say

"In the movie *The Secret Garden*, Colin has a disability. Throughout the course of the movie he becomes friends with Mary and Dickon. They are not afraid to get to know Colin because he is different."

Ask students

◆ What are some disabilities that people have?
◆ Have you ever known someone with a disability?
◆ Do you have a friend who has a disability?

Encourage the children to tell about their friends with disabilities. The nature of the particular disability is not important to the discussion. Guide students to discuss the friendships they have rather than the various disabilities their friends have.

Before the clip, say

"Everyone needs a friend. It doesn't matter if people have a disability or not; they simply need friends. Colin learns how important friends are from Mary and Dickon. Let's watch."

 ## Show the video clip.

Ask children who have a friend with a disability to answer these questions:
◆ How are you a friend to your friend with a disability?
◆ How is he or she a friend to you?
◆ Is this friendship different from your other friendships?

Say

"Friends are important to each of us. Let's stop and thank God for our friends now."

Encourage the children to pray for their friends. Guide the prayer to challenge children to build friendships with people even if they have a disability.

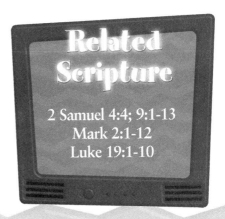

Related Scripture

2 Samuel 4:4; 9:1-13
Mark 2:1-12
Luke 19:1-10

Start time 2:56

Start cue
Singing from the stage: "We want to be like Peter Pan."

End time 7:46

End cue
Jack says, "Be sure to buy enough videotapes."

Clip summary

Peter Banning is a busy executive who disappoints his son Jack by not showing up at his ball game. Jack's dad tries to apologize, but Jack is still upset.

Materials

Cued video, TV, VCR

Ask students

◆ When playing a game, have you ever lost and been very upset about it?

Encourage the children to think of a ball game, board game, or playground game that they have lost. Allow several students to tell about the incident. Guide them to discuss how they felt. The most common feeling will be disappointment. Your students may say they were angry. Help them see that they were angry because they lost, but what they really felt was disappointment that they did not win. Have as many children participate as time permits.

Ask students

◆ Besides losing a game, when have you been disappointed?
◆ When have you seen a friend disappointed? Describe the circumstances.

Before the clip, say

"In this clip from the video *Hook*, Jack loses a game. He is disappointed, but the true cause of his disappointment may surprise you."

 ## Show the video clip.

Ask students

◆ How did Jack feel when his team lost the game?
◆ Do you think he blamed himself because he struck out?
◆ Was Jack more upset about striking out to lose the game or about his dad not being at the game?

Say

"Jack felt like his dad had let him down. He told him he would be there and then he wasn't."

Ask students

◆ How does it feel when an adult disappoints you?
◆ What are some situations when kids can be disappointed by adults?
◆ What are some ways kids can respond to the disappointment?

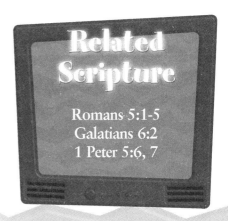

Related Scripture

Romans 5:1-5
Galatians 6:2
1 Peter 5:6, 7

Start time 29:57

Start cue
John Smith says, "It's called a helmet."

End time 32:80

End cue
The end of the song.

Clip summary

John Smith and Pocahontas teach each other their native ways of saying "hello." John explains what the English have planned for the "savages" and their land. Pocahontas is offended and tries to make John see that her people are just different—not inferior.

Materials

Cued video, TV, VCR

Say

"God created each of us differently. But we all are supposed to do one thing that is the same."

Ask students

◆ What did God create each of us to do?

Guide students to see that while each of us is a unique creation, God created every person who ever lived to love and honor him with his or her life.

Before the clip, say

"No matter when we live, what country we are from, or the color of our skin—God designed us to honor him with our lives.

"Pocahontas was an Indian in this country when the first English explorers came to develop a new world. The English explorers desired to make this country like their England. The Indians resisted. One of the English explorers, Captain John Smith, befriends Pocahontas. She tries to help him see that even though people are different, they are still important to one another."

 ## Show the video clip.

Ask students

◆ In what ways were Pocahontas and John Smith different from each other?

Guide the children to discuss such differences as the places they are from, the color of their skin, their gender, and how they say "hello."

Ask students

◆ Why is it important to recognize people's differences?
◆ Do you have any friends who look and think differently than you do? Tell about them.
◆ One of the lyrics Pocahontas sings is "We are all connected to each other in a circle, in a hoop, that never ends." How is this true?

Allow several students to respond.

Say

"No matter what color we are or where we are from, God created each of us for a very important reason."

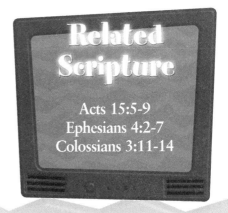

Related Scripture

Acts 15:5-9
Ephesians 4:2-7
Colossians 3:11-14

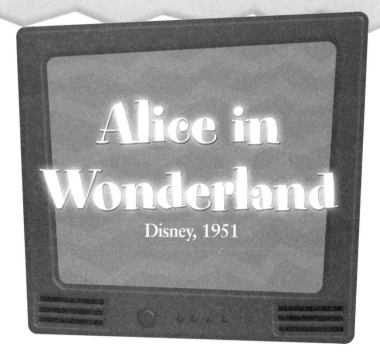

Start time 35:18

Start cue
The mome raths move to make an arrow.

End time 36:52

End cue
Alice ends her song.

Clip summary

Alice is in her make-believe Wonderland. She's trying to get out and go home. She sings about giving herself advice but not following it.

Materials

Cued video, TV, VCR, index cards, writing utensil

Ask students

◆ When you are about to do something that you know is wrong, what do you tell yourself?
◆ When you are going to do something right, how does it make you feel?
◆ Do you ever give yourself advice? What do you say?
◆ How often do you follow your advice: most of the time, sometimes, or never?

Before the clip, say

"When Alice is in Wonderland, she sings a song about giving herself advice, saying, 'I give myself very good advice, but I very seldom follow it.' Listen to her sing this song."

Show the video clip.

Ask students

◆ What is an example of some good advice that you give yourself?

Help students brainstorm good advice that they give themselves throughout the day. Challenge them to think of various situations in which they find themselves: for example, at home, school, with friends, with siblings and parents.

Say

"Let's think of some situations when children like you could get in trouble."

As students mention situations, write them down, one per index card. After you have 6-8 situations, give small groups of children one index card. Have each group think of good advice to give a child in that particular situation. Guide them to write the good advice on the back of their index card. Allow time for each small group to share its ideas with the whole group.

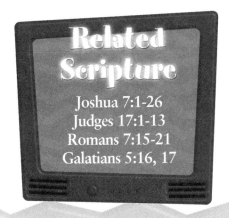

Related Scripture

Joshua 7:1-26
Judges 17:1-13
Romans 7:15-21
Galatians 5:16, 17

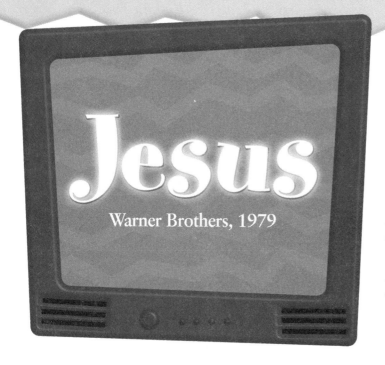

Warner Brothers, 1979

Start time 42:59

Start cue
The scene begins as the sun is rising and birds are chirping.

End time 44:81

End cue
Jesus says, "And lo, I am with you always, even unto the end of the world. Amen."

Clip summary

The women go to the tomb and see the burial cloth that had been around Jesus' body. Two angels appear and tell the women the good news of Jesus' resurrection. On hearing the report of the women, Peter runs to the tomb and discovers the truth for himself. Jesus appears to his disciples, then ascends into Heaven.

Materials

Cued video, TV, VCR, two-part plastic Easter eggs, slips of paper

Ahead of time, write each of the following questions on a slip of paper and place it inside a two-part egg:

◆ *Who went to the tomb to prepare Jesus' body for burial?*
◆ *What did the women find when they arrived at the tomb?*
◆ *Whom did the women see at Jesus' tomb?*
◆ *Whom did the women tell about what they saw at Jesus' tomb?*
◆ *Who appeared to the disciples and the other believers in the upper room?*
◆ *What did Jesus say when he saw the disciples and other believers after his resurrection?*

◆ *Why did Jesus say he had to die?*
◆ *How did Jesus leave the earth?*
◆ *What did Jesus say at the time he was leaving the earth?*

Say

"After Jesus died on the cross, there was a lot of confusion. The disciples and the other believers were very upset."

Ask students

◆ How do you think they felt?

Give each child a plastic egg. Instruct the children to open the eggs and one by one read and answer the questions inside.

Before the clip, say

"Some of these questions may be difficult for you. Let's watch the events following Jesus' death until he ascends into Heaven. Then we will try answering your questions again. Watch for the answer to your question."

 # Show the video clip.

Guide the children to read and answer their questions again after watching the video. If students still struggle with their answers, watch the video a second time, stopping at each question and discussing it as you go. The questions above are listed in the order in which they appear in the video clip.

Ask students

◆ What do you think the disciples thought happened when they went to the tomb and Jesus' body was gone?
◆ How do you think the disciples and other believers felt when Jesus appeared to them after his resurrection?
◆ How would you have felt if you had been at Jesus' ascension and had seen him raised into the sky?

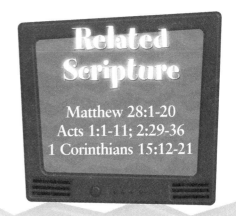

Related Scripture

Matthew 28:1-20
Acts 1:1-11; 2:29-36
1 Corinthians 15:12-21

Start time 19:04

Start cue

The toys are saying things like, "What is it?" and "Can you see it?"

End time 22:41

End cue

Woody says, "I'm still Andy's favorite toy."

Clip summary

Andy gets a new toy for his birthday. His other toys are envious of all the new toy's special features. Several of the toys compare Woody, an older toy, to Buzz, the new toy.

Materials

Cued video, TV, VCR, prepared 3" x 5" index cards

Ahead of time, you will need to write the following situations on 3" x 5" index cards:
◆ *John got a new pair of tennis shoes. Adam really wants a new pair just like them and considers stealing them.*
◆ *Sarah can sing, play the piano, and draw. Amanda doesn't think it is fair that Sarah can do all those things and she can't do any of them well.*
◆ *Dylan's dad left when he was little and he's lived with his mom. Dylan visits his friends' houses and realizes how much he's missed by not having a dad.*

Ask students

◆ Have you ever wished you had something someone else had?
◆ Have you ever wished you could be someone else?
◆ Have you ever wished you could have the abilities someone else has?

Before the clip, say

"A group of toys come to life in the movie *Toy Story*. Andy gets a new toy for his birthday. The other toys are getting to know him and learning about all the cool things he can do. They wish they could be like him. Let's watch."

 ## Show the video clip.

Say

"The toys were envious of Buzz Lightyear. They wanted to be like him. They wished they could have all the cool buttons, gadgets, and sounds he had. And he even had wings that helped him fly!"

Ask students

◆ When have you ever felt like the other toys did?
◆ How did Woody feel?
◆ When have you felt like Woody?

Guide the children in role-playing situations that involve envy. Have a child choose an index card and pick two others to act out the situation described on the card. Then, following each role play, discuss who was envious and why.

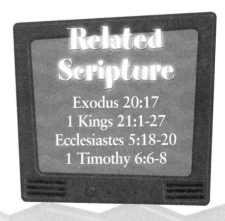

Related Scripture

Exodus 20:17
1 Kings 21:1-27
Ecclesiastes 5:18-20
1 Timothy 6:6-8

Start time 42:27

Start cue
Yoda says, "Use the force."

End time 44:36

End cue
Yoda says, "That is why you fail."

Clip summary

Luke Skywalker is training with Yoda, a Jedi master, to learn how to use "the force." He is struggling and disappointed with himself. Yoda encourages him to keep trying. Yoda uses the force to lift Luke's spacecraft out of the swamp and move it to dry land. Luke is shocked.

Materials

Cued video, TV, VCR, Bibles

Ask students

◆ True or false: "If you believe you can do it, you can do anything"?

Encourage the children to decide if they believe this statement is true or false. Have those who believe it is true stand on one side of the room and those who believe the statement is false stand on the other side of the room. Then discuss both sides.

On the one hand, it is important to have faith in yourself in order to accomplish anything. You must believe you can succeed in order to accomplish a goal. If you continually tell yourself "I can't," then you may not even try.

On the other hand, you may believe that you can jump from the Empire State Building and survive but if you jump, you will die. You may believe you can fly like a bird, but if you try, you will fail because people can't fly like birds.

Ask students

◆ Do you believe you can do anything?
◆ What limits you from doing anything?

Before the clip, say

"In the movie *The Empire Strikes Back*, Yoda is trying to teach Luke that he can use 'the force' to help him. Let's watch."

 Show the video clip.

Say

"Yoda told Luke at the end of this clip that he was failing because he didn't believe he could do it."

Ask students

◆ What does the Bible say about believing?
◆ What is the difference between believing in God's power and the power of "the force"?

Guide the children to read Matthew 17:20. Explain the importance of faith. It's not a magical trick but a supernatural by-product of believing in God's power.

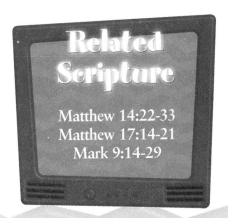

Related Scripture

Matthew 14:22-33
Matthew 17:14-21
Mark 9:14-29

Start time 9:32

Start cue
Marshall says, "Mom loved wild animals."

End time 10:58

End cue
Leon says, "Your daddy's coming home tomorrow."

Clip summary

Marshall is describing his family. His mom loves wild animals and has them in the house. Marshall has two brothers: one loves Hemingway, the other loves himself. Marshall's dad travels. And Leon, his dad's friend, lives with them.

Materials

Cued video, TV, VCR; full-body patterns of men, women, boys, girls, dogs, cats; construction paper, markers, scissors

Say

"God created families so that we would not have to live by ourselves. He wanted us to be able to share our lives with others."

Ask students

◆ Why do you think God thought families were so important to us?
◆ Why is it good for us to live in a family?

Say

"Every family in the world is different. There are no two families exactly alike. There are a lot of families with two kids and a mom and dad. Other children might live with only a mom or a dad, and some have no brothers or sisters—but even those families are not exactly alike. Each family is different because every single person God creates is different from everyone else."

Ask students

◆ What is unique about your family?
◆ What is one thing you love about your family?

Before the clip, say

"In the movie *Wild America*, Marshall describes his family. Let's watch."

 Show the video clip.

Ask students

◆ Who were the members of Marshall's family?
◆ What was unique about Marshall's family?

Be sure to discuss that Marshall's family had not only a mom, dad, and brothers, but that Leon was a special member of the family. Marshall's family also had pets. Help students make shaped outlines of their families. Using the patterns you provide, have the children trace each member of their family on one piece of construction paper. The children need to overlap the hands of the members of the family so that when they cut the shape out, their family is all one piece. Encourage students to include their pets. If they have pets other than a dog or cat, help them cut out a simple shape to represent their pet.

When the children have completed their family shapes, have each child display their family and tell about each person or animal.

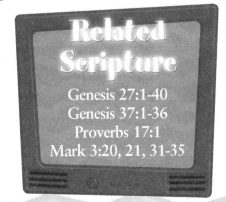

Related Scripture

Genesis 27:1-40
Genesis 37:1-36
Proverbs 17:1
Mark 3:20, 21, 31-35

Start time 15:72

Start cue
Kevin's dad says, "We made it."

End time 18:61

End cue
Uncle Frank says, "Look what you did, you little jerk."

Clip summary

Kevin gets left at home when his family goes on vacation. He wakes up one morning and the house is empty. His imagination starts to take over.

Materials

Cued video, TV, VCR

Ask students

◆ Have you ever been home alone? When?
◆ How did it feel to be home by yourself?
◆ What were you afraid of?
◆ Kevin was the boy in *Home Alone* who got left behind when his family went on a Christmas vacation. What was his first reaction when he discovered he was home by himself?

Before the clip, say

"Let's watch to see what Kevin does when he realizes he is home alone."

 Show the video clip.

Ask students

◆ What was Kevin's reaction when he discovered he was home by himself?

Guide the children to discuss that Kevin was afraid of being alone. He saw something strange and heard sounds in the basement that were scary. His mind started to run wild.

Ask students

◆ What can you do when you are afraid?
◆ What can you tell yourself when you are afraid?
◆ Who can you call when you are afraid?

Say

"God wants to help us when we are afraid. He cares about us very much. Because we are his children, he is concerned when we are afraid and need his help."

Ask students

◆ How can God help us?
◆ What do we need to do in order for God to help us when we are afraid?

Say

"God wants to help us no matter how we are feeling. Sometimes we are afraid. We also have other feelings that God can help us understand if we will just ask him."

Related Scripture

Psalm 27:1
Isaiah 41:10-13
Matthew 6:25-34
1 John 4:16-18

Ask students

◆ What are some other feelings God can help us cope with?

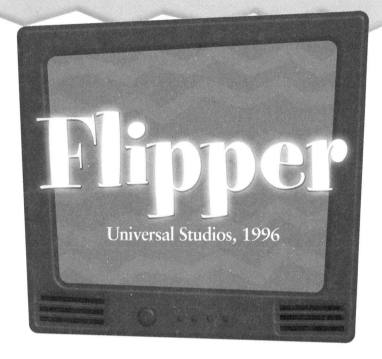

Start time 5:94

Start cue
Sandy gets off the island ferry.

End time 9:68

End cue
Sandy rolls over in bed.

Clip summary

Sandy arrives on an island to spend the summer with his uncle. He really doesn't want to be there and is disappointed that he will miss a concert while he is away. His uncle is about as excited about Sandy's arrival as Sandy is to be there.

Materials

Cued video, TV, VCR, poster board, markers

Before the clip, say

"In the movie *Flipper*, Sandy goes to stay with his uncle for the summer. He wanted to stay home so that he could go to a concert, but his mom sent him to spend some time with his uncle. Sandy is not looking forward to the summer. This video clip shows Sandy arriving on the island and meeting his uncle. Let's watch."

 Show the video clip.

Ask students

◆ From what you have seen, what do you know about Sandy?

Using a piece of poster board and some markers, ask students to make a list of what they observed about Sandy. Watch the clip a second time if necessary. Or discuss several things and watch it again. Be sure to include these items on their list:
◆ *Sandy's uncle did not care enough to pick him up at the dock.*
◆ *Sandy is not excited to be there.*
◆ *Sandy's parents are divorced.*
◆ *Sandy's mom paid his uncle to keep him for the summer.*
◆ *Sandy feels like his mom doesn't want him home for the summer.*

Ask students

◆ How do you think Sandy feels?
◆ How would you have felt if you had been in Sandy's shoes?

Guide the children to realize that Sandy is feeling lonely because he is in a new place, unwanted by his mom, and disappointed that he will miss the concert.

Ask students

◆ Have you ever felt like Sandy?

Allow the children to tell their stories as time permits.

Ask students

◆ What did you do to feel better?

Help students understand this is a great time to rely on God for strength, to pray, and to trust the Holy Spirit for guidance.

Related Scripture

Job 6:1–7:21
Psalm 43:5
John 11:17-36

Start time 14:15

Start cue
The matchmaker throws open the doors.

End time 17:40

End cue
Mulan's father: "When it blooms, it will be the most beautiful of all."

Clip summary

Mulan tries to make a good impression on the matchmaker so that she will find her a favorable mate, but everything goes wrong. It's a disaster! Mulan sings about wanting to fit in. Then her father reassures her.

Materials

Cued video, TV, VCR, enough apples for every child except one to have one, one banana, large basket

Place the apples and banana in the basket before the children arrive. Give every child except one an apple. Give that child the banana. Then discuss how the child feels who has a different type of fruit.

Ask the student

◆ Everyone but you has an apple. How does that make you feel?
◆ Would you rather have an apple than be the only one with a banana?

Say

"Sometimes we all feel like we are a little different from other people. We don't always feel like we fit in, do we? It feels as though we are the only person with a banana when everyone else has an apple."

Ask students

◆ What can we do when we feel this way?
◆ When is it a good thing to feel like we don't fit in?

Help the children see that it is good to feel like they don't fit in when others around them are doing something wrong. They don't want to give in to peer pressure and do the wrong thing.

Before the clip, say

"In this movie, Mulan doesn't feel like she fits in. She wants just to be herself. But the people around her want her to dress, act, and look like something she is not. One of the things Mulan says is, 'I can't hide who I am.'"

 ## Show the video clip.

Ask students

◆ What can you learn about fitting in from Mulan's father?
◆ How does his advice also apply to us?

Say

"We may not always fit in, but we always have a very important place on this earth. And God knows the importance of every single one of us. We are to take care of his world, bring others to him, and love him in a very special, unique way."

Related Scripture

Deuteronomy 26:18, 19
Luke 12:6, 7
1 Corinthians 15:10

Start time 18:84

Start cue
Professor says, "I've got it."

End time 21:77

End cue
The end of the song, when the tree laughs.

Clip summary

Larry crashes a tour boat, stranding everyone on an island. At first they are mad, but then decide to forgive him. A palm tree sings the "Lagoon Song," a song about forgiveness.

Materials

Cued video, TV, VCR, writing paper, pens or pencils

Say

"Forgiveness is very important—both for the person who needs to be forgiven and the one who is granting forgiveness. Jesus included both sides of forgiveness in his model prayer when he said, 'Forgive us our trespasses, as we forgive those who trespass against us.' It is good for us to forgive. It is also good for us to ask for forgiveness."

Ask students

◆ Do you think it is harder to forgive or to be forgiven? Why?

Say

"Describe a time when you had to forgive someone. Describe a time when you had to be forgiven by someone."

Allow plenty of time for students to tell their stories of forgiveness. Guide the conversation as necessary.

Before the clip, say

"In our video clip today, Larry finds himself in need of forgiveness. He has taken a group on a boat trip. He accidentally crashes the boat and strands them on an island. He thinks everyone is mad at him. They were, but now they want to forgive him. Let's watch and see what happens."

 ## Show the video clip.

Ask students

◆ How did Larry feel once he knew the others would forgive him?
◆ How do you think everyone else felt after they forgave Larry?

Say

"Forgiveness almost always makes everyone feel better."

Ask students

◆ Whom do you need to forgive?
◆ To whom do you need to say, "I'm sorry"?

Help each child think of a person to forgive or to ask for forgiveness. Distribute paper and writing utensils and have students write the person's name and description of the circumstances of forgiveness. Emphasize that no one else will see their papers. It is simply to help them remember to forgive or ask for forgiveness. Encourage the children to take their papers home and put them someplace prominent to remind them of the importance of forgiveness.

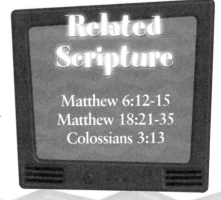

Related Scripture

Matthew 6:12-15
Matthew 18:21-35
Colossians 3:13

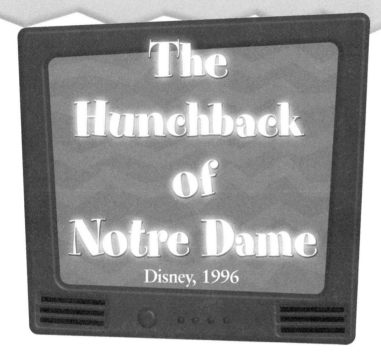

Start time 29:66

Start cue
Esmeralda says, "Wait! I want to talk to you."

End time 32:95

End cue
The captain says, "To have a friend like you."

Clip summary

The gypsy Esmeralda spends some time getting to know Quasimodo, the hunchback of Notre Dame. They quickly become friends. Esmeralda is not afraid of how Quasimodo looks, and Quasimodo is willing to help protect Esmeralda from the city guard.

Materials

Cued video, TV, VCR

Say

"Friends are very important to us, aren't they? Everyone wants and needs friends. God didn't design us to live alone in this world. That's why he created Eve for Adam. He wants us to have and enjoy our friends."

Ask students

◆ Who are some of your friends?
◆ Why do you like your friends?
◆ How did you get to know your friends?

Encourage students to talk about their friends. Have each child tell a story about a friend. Help them include information about how they met, what they like about their friends, and what kinds of things they do together.

Before the clip, say

"Quasimodo is a shy, physically-handicapped boy who takes care of the bells at the Notre Dame Cathedral. He meets a gypsy girl named Esmeralda.

"Watch this video clip and then we will talk more about friends. As you watch, look for how the friends treat each other."

Show the video clip.

Ask students

◆ Who were friends in the movie?

Students may suggest Esmeralda and Quasimodo, Esmeralda and the captain, Esmeralda and Jolly the goat, Quasimodo and the gargoyles. As they mention different friends, continue to question them about each friendship.

Ask students

◆ How do you know they were friends?
◆ What did they do because they were friends?

Guide the children to discuss characteristics of a good friend. Remind them of some of the things mentioned in the video clip. Quasimodo said Esmeralda was kind and good. They were willing to help each other.

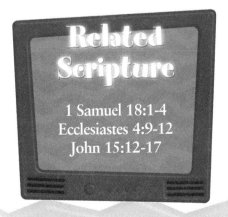

Related Scripture

1 Samuel 18:1-4
Ecclesiastes 4:9-12
John 15:12-17

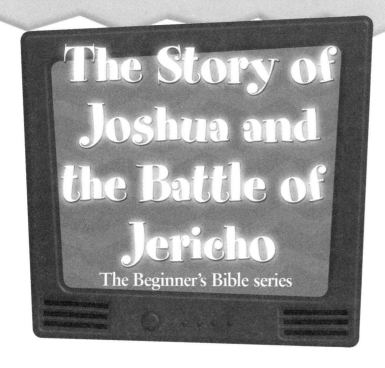

The Story of Joshua and the Battle of Jericho

The Beginner's Bible series

Start time 15:05

Start cue

Narrator: "On the morning of the seventh day, Joshua's people were restless."

End time 15:87

End cue

The Israelites are cheering.

Clip summary

Joshua and the Israelites have come into the land God has promised to them. They must defeat the people of Jericho in order to claim the promised land. Joshua and the people march around Jericho until the walls fall down.

Materials

Cued video, TV, VCR, bricks, black paint, thick opaque markers

Say

"God takes care of us in lots and lots of ways. He gives us food. He provides a place for us to live. He gives us parents to take care of us. Name at least ten other ways in which he shows his love for us."

Allow the children to take their time in answering how God cares for us. Guide them to suggest ways like providing the sun, moon, and rain; giving us freedom in our country; providing salvation through Jesus.

Before the clip, say

"God took care of his people, the Israelites, while they were slaves in Egypt and while they wandered in the wilderness. The Israelites knew God had promised them a land of their own. When they arrived in that land, there were other people there who called it 'home.' God told Joshua how to get the land for themselves. They were to march around the city for six days. On the seventh day, the people were to blow their horns and yell, and the walls would fall down. The city would be theirs. Let's watch and see what happens to the people on the seventh day."

 ## Show the video clip.

Ask students

◆ How did God take care of Joshua and the Israelites?
◆ What would have happened if Joshua had not obeyed God's instructions?

Say

"The Israelites probably had more faith in God once they saw the walls of the city of Jericho fall down. We should also have more trust in him after hearing this story."

Help the children make decorated bricks to remind them to trust God to take care of them. Ahead of time, spray-paint a brick for each child. The children can write a phrase on their bricks to remind them of God's care, such as: "Have faith in God," "God cares for me," or "Trust God."

Say

"These bricks will remind you of what God did for Joshua and the Israelites at Jericho and how much he cares for you today."

Related Scripture

Genesis 22:1-14
Joshua 5:13–6:27
1 Kings 17:1-24
James 1:16-18

Start time 7:05

Start cue

Narrator: "Well, Dave knew exactly what he had to do, so he went straight to King Saul and . . ."

End time 8:11

End cue

Narrator: ". . . but he knew God would be there with him."

Clip summary

Dave goes to King Saul to tell him that he will fight Goliath. Dave tells him even though he is young and Goliath is a giant, God is bigger.

Materials

Cued video, TV, VCR, Bible

Say

"There are probably a lot of times when you get frustrated that you are a kid. I remember when I was young . . ."

Tell a story of a time when you were a child and were frustrated with your ability, others' response to you, or a time when you decided to rely on God to help you.

Read 1 Timothy 4:12.

Before the clip, say

"Paul was telling Timothy that even though he was young, he could make a difference for God. God helps us and can use us for good even when we are young. Do you remember what David did when he was young? (*Lead the children to recall the story of David killing Goliath.*) Let's watch a video that may help us understand what he might have been feeling."

 ## Show the video clip.

Ask students

◆ You probably won't have to fight a giant like David did. What are some times that you may need God's help?

Direct your students to come up with times such as: dealing with family problems, standing up to a bully, being successful with difficult schoolwork, being brave against peer pressure. Make a list of the children's suggestions.

Guide the children to work in small groups. They will select a situation and rehearse their responses in that situation. Have the groups report to one another.

Say

"Just like Dave, we can learn that with God's help we can do big things too!"

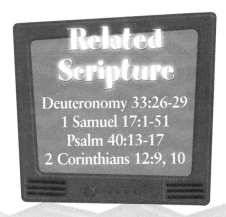

Related Scripture

Deuteronomy 33:26-29
1 Samuel 17:1-51
Psalm 40:13-17
2 Corinthians 12:9, 10

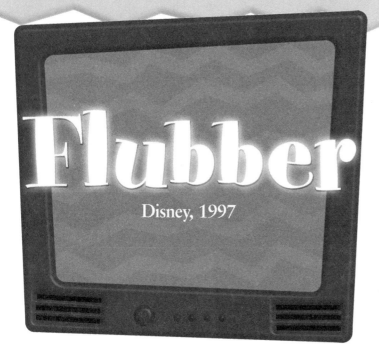

Start time 48:08

Start cue

Professor Brainard opens a pressure container holding Flubber.

End time 49:07

End cue

Flubber flies into Wilson's mouth, sending him into convulsions.

Clip summary

Professor Brainard and his fiancée Sara are trying to recover Flubber from a group of men who have stolen it. They use Flubber's special powers to help them. Flubber allows anything to bounce higher and faster—including Professor Brainard and Sara. When they spray Flubber on their hands, even the sinister men bounce off their fists.

Materials

Cued video, TV, VCR, small rubber balls

Before the clip, say

"In this movie, Flubber is a special make-believe substance a professor invents. It has special powers. Flubber bounces very high and very fast. In its liquid form, it can be sprayed on other things and make them bounce high and fast—even people. Some evil men want to use Flubber for themselves, so they steal it. But the professor and his girlfriend get it back. Let's watch to see how they do it."

 Show the video clip.

Ask students

◆ What did you learn about Flubber in the video clip?
◆ Is there really a substance like Flubber that will make those things happen?

Say

"Flubber is totally make-believe. By using Flubber, Professor Brainard could do special things that he could not do without it."

Ask students

◆ Did you know that there are special things you can do with God that you can't do without him?
◆ What are some of those things?

Guide the children to discuss ideas like their entry into Heaven, receiving forgiveness of sins, and the indwelling of the Holy Spirit.

Ask students

◆ How is God's power like Flubber?
◆ How is God's power different from Flubber?

Help the children see that Flubber is fun and make-believe, and that God's power is real. It is supernatural and available to those who follow God.

Ask students

◆ Why is God's power important to you?
◆ How do you use God's power?

Give each child a small rubber ball to remind him or her of God's power.

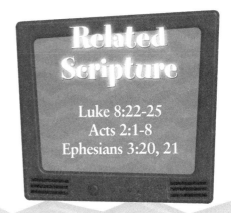

Related Scripture

Luke 8:22-25
Acts 2:1-8
Ephesians 3:20, 21

The Ten Commandments

Paramount, 1956

Start time 37:16
(on the second of two videos)

Start cue

Rameses says, "The God of Moses is a poor general to leave him no retreat."

End time 41:07

End cue

The Israelites say, "Thou art God."

Clip summary

The Israelites who are wandering in the wilderness under Moses' leadership come to a halt at the Red Sea. God holds back the waters for them to pass through and then releases the waters, drowning the Egyptian army.

Materials

Cued video, TV, VCR

Say

"Moses was the leader of the Israelites when they left Egypt to go to the promised land. The Egyptian army was chasing them in hopes of returning them to Egypt as slaves. The Israelites came to the Red Sea. The Egyptians were pursuing them. The Israelites needed to get across the Red Sea which would seem to be impossible."

Ask students

◆ Do you know what happened?
◆ Who caused the sea to part so that the Israelites could go to the other side?
◆ What happened when they arrived safely on the other side?

Before the clip, say

"The Egyptians also thought they could cross the Red Sea. But God had other plans. Let's watch to see what happened."

 Show the video clip.

Ask students

◆ Do you think more people believed in God's power or did not believe in God's power after they saw the waters divide? Why?
◆ What would make it easier to believe in God's power if you saw something like that?

Guide the children to understand that even though we may not have seen God's power demonstrated in such a vivid way, we can still believe in his mighty powers.

Say

"We have the Bible that tells us the wonderful stories of how God demonstrated his awesome powers."

Ask

◆ What are some other stories from the Bible that you can remember that show God's power?

Related Scripture

Jeremiah 32:26, 27
Mark 1:21-28
John 9:1-7
John 11:1-44

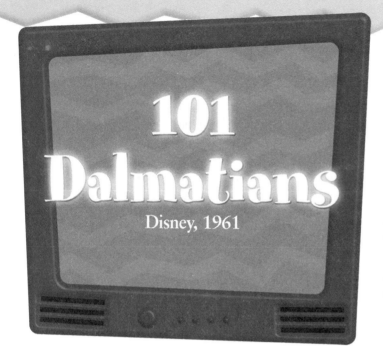

Start time 11:36

Start cue
Pongo says, "Oh, and that's Nanny, a wonderful cook and housekeeper."

End time 14:23

End cue
After Cruella leaves, Roger sings, "Cruella, Cruella De Vil."

Clip summary
Roger, Anita, and Nanny are introduced as nice, kind people. By contrast, Cruella De Vil is a villainess who obviously represents evil.

Materials
Cued video, TV, VCR

Ask students
◆ How would you define good?
◆ How would you define evil?

Help your students realize that good is what pleases God. Evil disappoints God and serves Satan.

Before the clip, say

"Some people do basically good things. And some people do mostly evil things. In the animated movie, *101 Dalmatians*, who does good? Let's watch to identify people who do good and people who do evil."

 ## Show the video clip.

Ask students

◆ Would you rather be like Anita and Roger or would you rather be like Cruella? Why?
◆ What did Cruella do later in the movie?
◆ Whose actions would please God?

Say

"Doing good is what pleases God. Sometimes the evil that people do looks fun and inviting, but it always leads to being destroyed."

Have the children work in small groups of three or four. Ask them to brainstorm some evil things that kids do. Then have the groups pantomime one evil action for the other groups to guess.

Ask students

◆ What are some evil things kids do that disappoint God?
◆ What are some good things kids do that please God?
◆ Is it easier or harder to do good and please God? Why? *(You may have a difference of opinion from some children on this question.)*
◆ How does it feel to do something that disappoints God? To do something that pleases God?

Related Scripture

Proverbs 4:18, 19
Luke 6:43-45
Galatians 6:7-10
1 Timothy 6:18

Start time 13:39

Start cue
Carface says, "Good-bye, Charlie."

End time 15:68

End cue
Charlie says, "Everything is so lovely here."

Clip summary
Charlie is killed by a car and goes to Heaven. He takes a mini-tour and learns a few things about his new home.

Materials
Cued video, TV, VCR, Bibles, art paper, drawing supplies

Before the clip, say
"The Bible has a lot to say about what Heaven will be like. But before we read some Bible verses, let's watch a video clip about Heaven. Charlie is a dog in the video, *All Dogs Go to Heaven*, who dies and goes to Heaven. Watch to see what he finds there."

 Show the video clip.

Say
"Now, let's read these Bible verses to see what God tells us about what Heaven will be like."

Help the children read and discuss these verses:
◆ *John 14:2*
◆ *2 Corinthians 5:1*
◆ *Revelation 21:4*

Ask students

◆ What is the same in the Bible as what Charlie experienced in the movie?
◆ What things are different?
◆ What is your favorite part about Heaven?

Say

"Heaven is probably going to be very different from what Charlie experienced. One thing is for sure—it is more wonderful than we can possibly imagine."

Ask students

◆ Does God have a watch for each one of us like the one Charlie had?

Students will probably answer "no." Discuss the fact that God knows everything about us—even the number of days that we will live on the earth. He may not have a watch for every one of us, but he knows how long we will live.

Ask students

◆ What are you looking forward to when you get to Heaven?

Distribute the paper and drawing supplies. Ask the children to draw pictures of what they think Heaven may look like. Then have them display their art and describe the pictures to one another as time permits.

Related Scripture

1 Corinthians 2:9, 10
Revelation 4:1–5:14
Revelation 21:1–22:6

Start time 5:39

Start cue
The beginning of the movie.

End time 9:67

End cue
The queen says, "Bring back her heart in this."

Clip summary

The queen's magic mirror tells her that Snow White is more beautiful than she is. The queen is so jealous she commissions a servant to kill Snow White. Snow White is introduced and meets the prince.

Materials

Cued video, TV, VCR, dictionary, small inexpensive mirrors for each child, adhesive-strip magnets

Ask students

◆ What is jealousy?

Have a child look up the word "jealousy" in the dictionary.

Ask students

◆ Have you ever been jealous?

Encourage several children to describe a time they were jealous. If the children struggle to think of instances of jealousy, prompt them with these situations: another child getting new clothes or shoes, a sibling's birthday gifts, a friend's privileges.

Ask students

◆ Who was jealous of Snow White in the movie *Snow White and the Seven Dwarfs*?
◆ Why was the queen jealous?
◆ Because of her jealousy, what did the queen want to do to Snow White?

 ## Show the video clip.

Ask students

◆ When you are jealous, what can you tell yourself about it?
◆ Is it wrong to be jealous?

Guide students to think of some constructive things to do with their jealous thoughts: thank God for what you have, become a friend, respond with love, avoid opportunities to be jealous.

Then, give each child a small mirror with a magnetic strip adhered to the back of it. Instruct students to place the mirror someplace where they will see it often: for example, their school lockers, the refrigerator at home, in their rooms.

Say

"When you see this mirror, let it remind you to turn your jealous thoughts into thoughts of love and thankfulness."

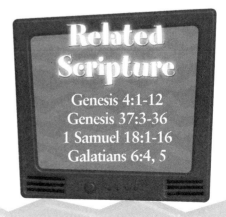

Related Scripture

Genesis 4:1-12
Genesis 37:3-36
1 Samuel 18:1-16
Galatians 6:4, 5

Jesus' Death, Sacrifice

Start time 18:28

Start cue
The Queen says, "Bala, you must encourage the troops."

End time 18:98

End cue
The general says, ". . . to die for the colony."

Clip summary

The ants are preparing to go into battle with the termites. The general of the ant army is giving a pep talk to his troops about sacrifice.

Materials

Cued video, TV, VCR, poster board, marker

Before class, make a poster with the general's quote written on it: "Sacrifice: To some it is just a word. To others it is a code. A soldier knows that the life of an individual ant doesn't matter. What matters is the colony. He's willing to live for the colony, to fight for the colony, to die for the colony."

Ask students

◆ Why did Jesus come to live on the earth?

Accept several answers from the children: such as to show us how to live, to teach us about God, to die on the cross.

Say

"Jesus' life was very important for us, as were his death and resurrection!"

Ask students

◆ Why are Jesus' death and resurrection important to us?
◆ Jesus died as a sacrifice for the sins of the world. What does the word "sacrifice" mean?

Discuss the meaning of sacrifice. Use Scripture references or a dictionary as needed.

Before the clip, say

"In the movie *Antz,* the general of the ant army is talking to his troops right before a battle. He talks to them about sacrifice. Let's watch."

 ## Show the video clip.

Ask students

◆ What did the general say about *sacrifice?*
◆ The general said the life of one ant is not as important as the whole colony. Do you think he is right? Why?

Show the poster with the general's quote written on it.

Say

"This is what the general said. We are going to rewrite it so that it matches something Jesus might have said about sacrifice."

Help students cross out some words in the phrase to change the general's quote to something Jesus might have said. For example: "Sacrifice: To some it is just a word; to others it is a purpose. God knows that the life of his Son can be laid down. What matters is all of mankind. His Son is willing to live for mankind, to fight for mankind, to die for mankind."

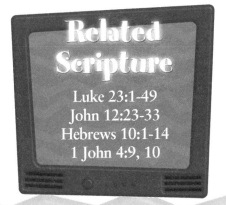

Related Scripture

Luke 23:1-49
John 12:23-33
Hebrews 10:1-14
1 John 4:9, 10

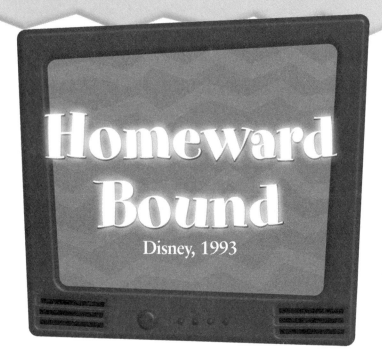

Start time 13:28

Start cue
The family vehicle arrives at the farm.

End time 16:16

End cue
Shadow says, "You'll come back. I know you'll come back."

Clip summary

The kids have to leave their two dogs and cat at the farm while they make a temporary move. The kids say good-bye to their animals. The animals talk about missing the kids, and the kids discuss being separated from their pets.

Materials

Cued video, TV, VCR

Say

"We have all felt lonely at some time in our lives."

Describe a time when you were lonely. Explain why you felt the way you did and what you did to feel better. Emphasize the importance of doing something about your loneliness.

Before the clip, say

"We are going to watch a video clip that will remind us how it feels to be lonely. A family is moving to another city because their dad's job is temporarily moving. The kids are going to have to leave their pets behind because there won't be room for them. They take their dogs and cat to a friend's farm for several weeks. The kids don't want to leave their animals—and it appears that the animals don't want to be left either! Let's watch."

 ## Show the video clip.

Ask students

◆ Have you ever felt lonely?

Encourage students to tell their stories of loneliness. Ask questions to stimulate their storytelling. Guide them to explain why they felt lonely and what they did about it.

Say

"God wants to help us when we feel lonely."

Ask students

◆ How can God help us deal with loneliness?
◆ Whom can God use to help us when we feel lonely?
◆ What will you do the next time you feel lonely?

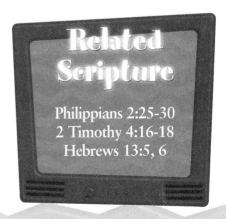

Related Scripture

Philippians 2:25-30
2 Timothy 4:16-18
Hebrews 13:5, 6

Start time 25:23

Start cue

Princess Buttercup says, "I know who you are. Your cruelty reveals everything."

End time 26:63

End cue

Wesley and Buttercup come to rest at the bottom of the hill.

Clip summary

Princess Buttercup thinks her life's love, Wesley, has been killed by pirates. She is now engaged to marry the prince. Wesley, disguised as a pirate, rescues her from kidnappers and talks to her about her former love. She has not yet recognized him.

Materials

Cued video, TV, VCR, Bibles

Say

"We are going to talk about being in love and getting married."

Expect the children to groan and moan about discussing such a "gross" topic.

Say

"As you get older, you will start dating so that you can get to know guys or girls better. You will enjoy spending time with someone who is the opposite gender from you. You will find out that guys are different from girls and girls are different from guys. Believe it or not, you will have fun getting to know other people!"

Ask students

◆ How would you explain dating to someone who had never heard of it?
◆ What do you think it would be like to fall in love when you are in high school?
◆ Do you know any high school students who are in love? Describe what it is like.

Help students talk about dating and falling in love. Guide them to discuss such things as double dates, getting to know a boyfriend or girlfriend, and spending time together in the context of junior high or high school. They are more likely to imagine dating rather than marriage. Some of the children may have older siblings who are in this age range and have already started to date. Others may be interested in exploring concepts like courtship rather than dating.

Ask students

◆ What will you like about dating?
◆ What will you not like about dating?

Before the clip, say

"Watch this video clip from *The Princess Bride*. Listen for the way in which Princess Buttercup and Wesley describe love."

 ## Show the video clip.

Then rewind and play the clip a second time. Instruct the students to yell "stop" when they hear something said about love. Push "pause" and discuss the point from the video. Continue playing and pausing the video until you have finished the clip.

Say

"One day you will start dating. God has given us lots of guidelines for how to love someone. Let's read some of them."

Guide the children to read and discuss passages about love and marriage. Here are a few: 1 Corinthians 13:4-8; Ephesians 5:22-33; 1 Peter 3:1-7.

Related Scripture

Genesis 24:1-58
1 Corinthians 13:4-8
1 John 4:16-19

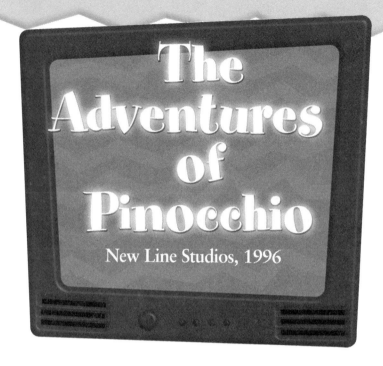

Start time 19:95

Start cue

Teacher: "Would someone please like to tell us of a characteristic which separates humans from the rest of the animal kingdom?"

End time 22:68

End cue

The classroom door closes in Pinocchio's face.

Clip summary

Pinocchio lies for the first time: he tells the schoolteacher that he was not involved in a scuffle with two boys. His nose begins to grow with each new lie he tells and shrinks with each acknowledgment of a lie. Everyone is surprised to see his nose get longer and longer.

Materials

Cued video, TV, VCR

Say

"No one is happy with us when we lie. Lying hurts a lot of people, including the one who told the lie. God feels so strongly that we should not lie that he made it one of his Ten Commandments."

Ask students

◆ Do you know the story of Pinocchio?
◆ What happened to Pinocchio when he lied?

Before the clip, say

"Let's watch as Pinocchio tells his first lie. He doesn't know that anyone will find out he is lying. He thinks he can get away with it."

 ## Show the video clip.

Ask students

◆ What led to Pinocchio's lie?
◆ Would it be easy or difficult to lie if you were in Pinocchio's position?
◆ How did one lie lead to another lie for Pinocchio?
◆ Has this ever happened to someone you know?

Guide the children to tell stories of lies gone bad. Help them see that lying is never a good choice. And even though their noses don't grow, they always run the risk of being found out and hurting other people.

Ask students

◆ What could Pinocchio have done rather than tell a lie?

Help students come up with several options other than lying.

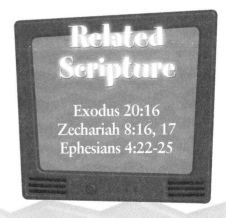

Related Scripture

Exodus 20:16
Zechariah 8:16, 17
Ephesians 4:22-25

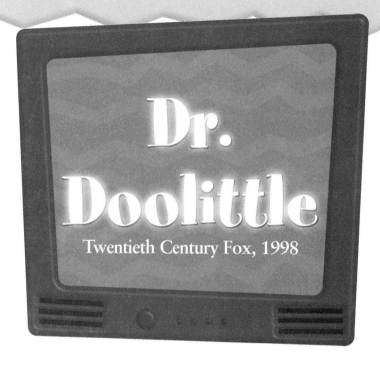

Start time 36:78

Start cue

Mia says, "This is where you live and this is where you exercise."

End time 38:12

End cue

Mia says, "See you inside."

Clip summary

Mia is upset because her dad doesn't seem very interested in her. She knows he loves her; she just thinks he doesn't *like* her. Her grandfather encourages her. Finally, Mia's dad talks with her to let her know that he *likes* her and he *loves* her.

Materials

Cued video, TV, VCR

Say

"Sometimes parents have a hard time expressing what they are thinking. Their actions may not always tell us how they really feel about us. Moms and dads can be very busy and not realize that we need them."

Ask students

◆ How have your feelings been hurt when your mom didn't give you some attention?
◆ How have your feelings been hurt when you needed some attention from your dad?
◆ Did your mom or dad know that you felt hurt?

Before the clip, say

"Many times we don't know that our actions can hurt other people. This can happen even to moms and dads. Let's watch and see what happens with Mia and her dad in the movie *Dr. Doolittle*."

 ## Show the video clip.

Ask students

◆ How did Mia feel when she was talking to her grandpa?
◆ Have you ever felt like Mia did about your mom or dad?

Take time for several children to tell about their feelings and what prompted them to feel the way they did. Encourage the children by reassuring them.

Ask students

◆ How do you think Mia felt after she talked with her dad in the car?
◆ Have you ever had a conversation like that with your mom or dad?

Again, have several of the children tell about their conversations with a parent. Guide students with positive statements, pointing out the parent's love and concern for the child.

Say

"Even though parents are very busy and at times have trouble giving their children lots of attention, that doesn't mean that they love their children any less."

Related Scripture

Psalm 78:1-7
Proverbs 6:20-23
Colossians 3:20, 21

Start time 12:61

Start cue
Jessie says, "'Scuse me."

End time 15:40

End cue
Two boys are spray-painting graffiti on a lab in the dark.

Clip summary

Jessie and his friends are bumming money to buy food. They take table scraps from a restaurant, then they steal a cake from a caterer. They end up running from the police and vandalizing a building.

Materials

Cued video, TV, VCR

Say

"We can convince our friends to do good. We can also persuade our friends to do things that are wrong."

Ask students

◆ How can we influence our friends to do what is good?
◆ How do our friends influence us to do things that are wrong?
◆ What are some things that are wrong that someone could convince their friends to participate in?

Encourage your students to name actions ranging from lying to participating in illegal activities like smoking, drinking, and taking drugs.

Before the clip, say

"As you watch this group of friends from the movie *Free Willy*, think about how they are influencing each other. Look for ways in which they are encouraging each other to do good and ways in which they are convincing each other to do some things that are wrong."

Show the video clip.

After viewing the clip, guide the children to discuss each episode of doing wrong: how the circumstances presented themselves, who made the decision to act, and how everyone else got involved. Help students see that their friends can be swayed by them to do right or wrong. And, more importantly, they also can be pulled to do right or wrong by their friends' influence.

Ask students

◆ What are some times when it is important to stand up for what is right?
◆ Have you ever had a friend convince you to do something that was wrong? Describe it.
◆ How did you feel afterwards?
◆ Have you ever convinced a friend to do something that was right? Describe it.
◆ How did you feel afterwards?

Say

"Sometimes it is hard for us to stand up to our friends, but it is an important thing to do. Often, you find out when you stand up for what you believe that another friend was feeling the same way too."

Related Scripture

Exodus 23:1, 2
Matthew 13:24-30
Luke 17:1-3
1 Corinthians 15:33, 34

Start time 20:45

Start cue
Jr. says, "Well, I was hoping you'd ask."

End time 21:46

End cue
The end of the song.

Clip summary
Larry, Bob, and Jr.—as Rack, Shack, and Benny—learn that sometimes God needs us to stand up for what we know is right. The song "Stand Up" reminds children to stand up for what is right by drawing strength from God's Word and their parents' guidance.

Materials
Cued video, TV, VCR

Ask students
◆ Have you ever known what was right but been tempted by other kids to do what was wrong?

Say
"That's called peer pressure. Other people put pressure on us all the time to do something wrong."

Give a specific example of peer pressure by telling about a time you felt peer pressure when you were a child. Use an illustration your group of children can relate to.

Before the clip, say

"God wants us to stand up and be strong when we are faced with peer pressure. Let's listen to this song to remind us to stand up to peer pressure."

 ## Show the video clip.

Write down these situations for small groups of three to five students to discuss. Ask each group to come up with two ways to stand up for what is right in each situation. Give the children enough time to work together. Then discuss their responses and other possible solutions.

Situation #1

A classmate offers you a cigarette in front of some of your friends. One of your friends is already smoking.

Situation #2

Your sister wants you to lie to your mom about where she is. She already did something nice for you today.

Situation #3

A friend wants you to skip school and walk to the mall. You'll be back in time to catch the bus home.

Rewind the video clip and play it again, encouraging the children to sing the song along with Rack, Shack, and Benny.

Related Scripture

Psalm 40:6-8
Psalm 135:15-18
Isaiah 44:9-19
Daniel 3:1-30

Start time 49:19

Start cue
Scarecrow asks, "What about the heart that you promised Tin Man?"

End time 50:36

End cue
Dorothy says, "Oh, they're all wonderful."

Clip summary

Dorothy, Scarecrow, Cowardly Lion, and Tin Man are talking to the Wizard about their desires: in their respective order, they want to go home, get a brain, courage, and a heart. The Wizard gives Scarecrow a diploma, Cowardly Lion a medal, and Tin Man a heart clock. He is just about to talk to Dorothy about going home to Kansas.

Materials

Cued video, TV, VCR

Ask students

◆ How many of you have seen *The Wizard of Oz*?
◆ What are the main characters looking for in the movie?
◆ Where do they go to find it?

Help the children recall that the Scarecrow wants a brain, the Cowardly Lion wants to have courage, the Tin Man wants a heart, and Dorothy just wants to go home to Kansas. They go on a trek to find the Wizard who can grant their wishes.

Before the clip, say

"Let's see what happens when they finally reach the Wizard."

 Show the video clip.

Say

"The Scarecrow, Cowardly Lion, Tin Man, and Dorothy all wanted things that money can't buy. Knowledge, courage, tenderness, and a home were very important to them."

Ask students

◆ What are some things you want that money can't buy?

Steer the children to name some intangible things that are important to them — things like caring parents, a loving home, self-esteem.

Ask students

◆ Since we don't have a Wizard like Dorothy and her friends, to whom can we go and ask for the things that we want?
◆ Will God always give us what we ask for?

Say

"God loves us and wants to bless us. He will always take good care of us."

Related Scripture

Luke 18:1-8
1 John 5:13-15

Start time 10:85

Start cue
The kids are playing ball in their yard.

End time 13:57

End cue
Angus pours food into Yellow's dog bowl.

Clip summary

Angus and Silas adopt a stray dog and name him Yellow. The dog tries to retrieve the boys' baseball and ruins a bedsheet on the line in the process. A neighbor dog barks at Angus and Yellow tries to get to him, dragging Silas through a mud puddle. The dog chases and kills a chicken. Angus wants to keep the dog but his parents are against it. Angus' parents finally give in but make sure he understands the dog is his responsibility.

Materials

Cued video, TV, VCR

Say

"If you've ever owned a pet, you know that they need to be taken care of. Different pets need different kinds of care."

Ask students

◆ If you had a cat, what would you need to do to take care of him?
◆ If you had a bird, what would it need from you?
◆ What would you need to do if you had a snake for a pet?
◆ How about a guinea pig, hamster, or fish?
◆ It's important to take care of our pets. And you have to do it every day. What would happen if you didn't take care of your pet every day?
◆ Taking care of a pet requires that you be responsible. What does it mean to be responsible?

Discuss responsibility in the context of taking care of pets. Pets need food and water. Some need to be exercised. Some need their habitats cleaned.

Before the clip, say

"Watch this video clip and see what you can learn about being responsible."

Show the video clip.

Ask students

◆ What will Angus have to do to take care of Yellow?
◆ What did Angus' parents say about responsibility?

Say

"Sometimes responsibility means you have to say 'I'm sorry' or 'That was my fault.'"

Ask students

◆ What did Yellow do that Angus has to take responsibility for?
◆ What should Angus do because of what Yellow did?

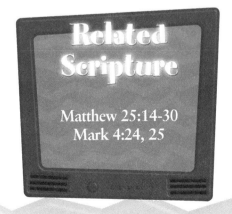

Related Scripture

Matthew 25:14-30
Mark 4:24, 25

Start time 8:94

Start cue

The son says, "I've been acting so foolishly."

End time 9:54

End cue

Narrator: "And the son realized how much his father loved him."

Clip summary

Jesus' parable of the prodigal son is found in Luke 15. The son leaves home to experience the world, loses everything, and must go back home to his father. His father is excited to see him and throws a celebration party. This parable is a picture of God's love for us through salvation.

Materials

Cued video, TV, VCR, work hat, work boots, a farm tool, coins and dollar bills, pig stuffed animal, "Welcome Home" banner made from shelf paper

Ask students

◆ Have you ever wanted to run away from home?
◆ What made you want to run away?
◆ If you did run away, what made you come back home?

Before the clip, say

"Jesus told a story about a son who wanted to run away from home. His dad gave him some of his inheritance and the son left. He wanted to see what the world was like. Let's read about what happened to him." *(Read Luke 15:11-19.)*

Ask students

◆ How do you think the father felt when his son left with his inheritance?
◆ Do you think he knew his son would make mistakes?
◆ Did he quit loving his son?

Say

"The father knew what would happen to his son, but he never quit loving him."

 ## Show the video clip.

Ask students

◆ How did the father feel when his son returned home?
◆ How do you think this made the son feel?

Help the children retell the story using the props you provide.

Say

"This story is a parable Jesus told. God is like the father. We are like the son. God knows that we do things wrong; we sin. God is very excited when we come back to him."

Ask students

◆ What do we do when we come back to God?

Use this opportunity to discuss salvation and the steps to take to come back to God.

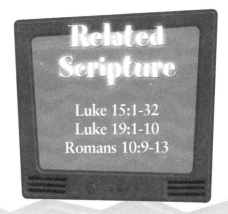

Related Scripture

Luke 15:1-32
Luke 19:1-10
Romans 10:9-13

Start time 43:49

Start cue

Madeline and Pepito are asleep. Madeline says, "I can do anything."

End time 45:65

End cue

The kidnappers are in the water surrendering to the police.

Clip summary

Madeline and Pepito have been kidnapped. They figure out a way to escape. They are successful and their captors are arrested.

Materials

Cued video, TV, VCR

Say

"We all have times in our lives when we think we cannot do something. When we are little, we may think that we will never be able to ride a two-wheeled bike or rollerblades without falling over, but we soon learn that we can do those things if we practice. Even though it is difficult, we can be successful if we just try."

Ask students

◆ What are some things you didn't think that you could ever do that you discovered you *can* do?
◆ Why did you think you wouldn't be successful?

Say

"Sometimes we are afraid of trying something new. We may look silly, or we may not do it right and fail."

Ask students

◆ What are some other reasons people may not feel confident about trying something?
◆ What are some things that kids may be hesitant to try?
◆ What may make kids feel like they can't do something?

Before the clip, say

"Madeline and Pepito were in a bad situation and they needed to know that they could be successful. They had been kidnapped by men from a circus. In the video clip, they are tied up and locked in a truck. They need to figure out what to do to get free. Let's see what happens."

 ## Show the video clip.

Ask students

◆ You probably have never been kidnapped by men in the circus. What has happened to you where you needed to tell yourself, "I can do anything," like Madeline did?

Give several children the opportunity to tell their stories.

Say

"You can do almost anything that you decide you want to do. When you have God on your side, he will help you be successful. He wants what is best for you. With God, anything is possible."

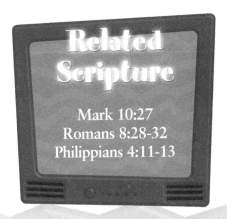

Related
Scripture

Mark 10:27
Romans 8:28-32
Philippians 4:11-13

Start time 45:86

Start cue
Music and fireworks stop.

End time 46:78

End cue
Julie says, "So, today we're going to make our own pasta primavera."

Clip summary

A group of boys at a fitness camp decide to binge on every morsel of food they can get their hands on. A camp counselor encourages the boys to act responsibly, respect themselves, and demonstrate some self-control.

Materials

Cued video, TV, VCR

Ask students

◆ What are some things that you love to do?
◆ How much time in one week do you spend participating in these activities?

Help students come up with such things as watching TV, playing video or computer games, talking to friends, and participating in sports.

Say

"There are a number of ways in which we spend our time that are good for us. There are also lots of ways in which we spend our time that are not healthy. And, there are some things that we do that are okay as long as we don't do them *all* the time."

Ask students

◆ What are some things that are okay for us to do but should be stopped at some point?

Guide the children to discuss such activities as video and computer games, watching TV, or eating.

Say

"There are times when too much of a good thing is no longer good for us. For instance, if we watch too much TV, we limit the time that we spend with our families and friends."

Ask students

◆ What happens when someone spends too much time playing video and computer games?
◆ What happens when someone eats too much?

Before the clip, say

"In the movie *Heavyweights*, a group of boys at camp learn what happens when they eat too much. Let's watch."

 Show the video clip.

Ask students

◆ What is self-control?
◆ How did the boys show that they did not have self-control?
◆ What might they have done if they'd shown some self-control?
◆ How does self-control show that you respect yourself?
◆ When do kids like you need to show some self-control?

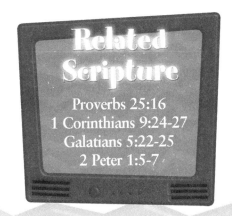

Related Scripture

Proverbs 25:16
1 Corinthians 9:24-27
Galatians 5:22-25
2 Peter 1:5-7

Start time 28:12

Start cue
A little girl says to Moses, "Sit with me."

End time 32:59

End cue
God says, "I shall be with you, Moses."

Clip summary

Moses has just fled Egypt and isn't feeling very good about himself. His father-in-law, Jethro, encourages him to find his value from God. Moses encounters God at the burning bush and learns of God's plan for him to lead the Israelites out of Egypt.

Materials

Cued video, TV, VCR

Before the clip, say

"I'm going to read several statements about Moses and I want you to tell me if he felt good about himself or if he felt like a loser. All of these things happened to Moses during his lifetime.

"After I read each statement, if you think Moses felt good about himself, stand up. If you think Moses felt like a loser, sit down on the floor."

As you read each statement about Moses' life, have the children respond accordingly.

- Moses was raised as a member of Pharaoh's family in the palace.
- Moses discovered that he wasn't an Egyptian. He was an Israelite like the Egyptian slaves.
- Moses killed an Egyptian for the way he was treating an Israelite.
- Moses ran away from Egypt after he committed murder.
- God chose Moses to be the leader of his people, the Israelites.
- Moses had to go back to Egypt and the Pharaoh.
- Moses led thousands and thousands of Israelites out of Egypt to freedom.

Say

"In the movie *The Prince of Egypt*, Jethro sings a song to help Moses feel better about himself. Let's listen to Jethro's song."

 Show the video clip.

Stop the clip at the end of Jethro's song (cue 30:09).

Ask students

- What was Jethro's advice to Moses?
- What does it mean to look "through Heaven's eyes"?
- If Moses were to look at his life through Heaven's eyes, what might he see?
- Do you think it mattered to God if Moses was wealthy or strong? Why or why not?
- If you looked at your life through Heaven's eyes, what might you see?

Say

"God chose Moses to be his special leader to save the Israelites. God appeared to Moses in a bush that was on fire but not burning up—and he talked to him. Let's watch to see what happened."

 Show the remainder of the video clip.

Related Scripture

Genesis 1:26-31
Judges 7:1-25
Psalm 139:13-16
Romans 12:1-8

Start time 14:36

Start cue
The camp counselor says, "Okay, we got ourselves a challenger!"

End time 15:71

End cue
The twins shake hands.

Clip summary
One of the first of the twins' encounters in the film is during a fencing match with each other. One twin wins. The loser pulls the winner into a tub of water. The camp counselor must coax the two girls to shake hands.

Materials
Cued video, TV, VCR, poster board, marker

 ## Show the video clip.

Ask students
◆ How many of you would like to take your brother or sister on in fencing?
◆ Would you be kind and fair or would you fight dirty?
◆ Would you willingly shake hands after the match or would someone have to make you?

Say
"Describe a time when you felt like you were fencing with your brother or sister. It

might be a time you were arguing or disagreeing about something. It could be a time when you did not feel very close to each other."

Have several children respond.

Ask students

◆ Was there a winner?
◆ Was the loser a sore loser like the girl in the video clip?
◆ What did it take for the two of you to shake hands and call it quits?

Say

"Having a brother or sister can be a wonderful experience. It can also be very difficult at times. Let's make a list of what's great and what's difficult about having brothers and sisters."

Help the children make a list of the pluses and minuses of having siblings. Be sure to list far more positives that negatives.

Ask students

◆ What can you do to work at your relationship with your brother or sister?

Related Scripture

Genesis 29:14–30:24
Genesis 37:1-36
John 7:1-5

Start time 16:12

Start cue

Pooh is rolling around in a mud puddle.

End time 18:56

End cue

Back in the mud puddle, Pooh spits out a bee.

Clip summary

Pooh disguises himself as a rain cloud in order to sneak into the bees' honey source. He inadvertently stirs up the bees enough for them to swarm and begin chasing him.

Materials

Cued video, TV, VCR, dictionary, Bible

Ask students

◆ What is sin?

Look up the definition of "sin" in the dictionary: an offense against the law of God. Help students understand the technical definition of sin.

Next, look up "sin" in a concordance and help students understand what the Bible says about sin. Use such references as Romans 6:23 and 1 John 1:7-10.

Ask students

◆ What are some examples of sins?
◆ What are some sins that children like you commit?

Allow several students to respond.

Before the clip, say

"Winnie the Pooh loves honey because he is a bear. He steals the honey from the bees. Let's watch to see what happens to Pooh."

 Show the video clip.

Ask students

◆ What can we learn about sin from Winnie the Pooh?
◆ What happened to Pooh because he stole the honey?
◆ How did Pooh get Christopher Robin involved?

Help the children understand that because Pooh stole the honey, it upset the bees and caused them to chase him and Christopher Robin.

Ask students

◆ How did Pooh's stealing the honey put him in danger?
◆ How is sinning dangerous to us?
◆ What were the consequences of Pooh's stealing the honey?
◆ What are some consequences when we sin?
◆ How does God protect us from sin?
◆ How does God help us to avoid sinning?

Say

"God wants us to avoid sinning and to follow the rules that he made for us. It's important to him that we love him by obeying his rules."

Ask students

◆ What are some rules that God made for us?

Say

"God gave us rules to follow because he loves us."

Related Scripture

Exodus 2:11-17
2 Samuel 11:1-27
Psalm 51:1-12
1 John 1:7-10

The Fiendish Works of Dr. Fear

BibleMan series

1st clip start time
13:99

Start cue
Miles: "Ready the chamber, my friend . . ."

End time 14:40

End cue
BibleMan: "I'll take the tunnel back. Track me."

Clip summary
Miles becomes BibleMan—a superhero destined to fight Satan and his demons with the Word of God—by putting on the armor of God found in Ephesians 6:10-18.

2nd clip start time 18:87

Start cue
Dr. Fear says, "Presenting the battle of the ages."

End time 20:29

End cue
Blackout

Clip summary
Dr. Fear and BibleMan battle one another. BibleMan fights back by quoting Scripture.

Materials
Cued video, TV, VCR, Bibles, butcher paper, pencils, markers

Say

"One of the most important ways we can fight Satan is to wear God's armor."

Read Ephesians 6:10-18 and discuss how the armor of God protects us against temptation.

Before the first clip, say

"There is a fictional superhero named BibleMan who wears God's armor to win battles against his darkest foe, the devil. Let's take a look."

 ## Show the first video clip.

Ask students

◆ Why would BibleMan need a belt of truth in order to defeat Satan?

Ask this question with each piece of armor: breastplate of righteousness, shield of faith, helmet of salvation, and sword of the Spirit. Explain as necessary.

Before the second clip, say

"BibleMan uses one more means of defense against his enemy. Let's see what that is. We are going to watch BibleMan defeat Dr. Fear."

Fast-forward the video and show the second clip.

Ask students

◆ What did BibleMan use to help him defeat Dr. Fear?

Say

"We can also use Scripture in order to resist Satan's temptation. That's what Jesus did!"

Guide the children to make book covers for their Bibles using the butcher paper and markers. Have them include in their designs one of the Scriptures BibleMan quoted: 1 John 4:4; 2 Timothy 1:7; and Proverbs 3:26.

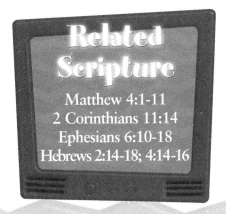

Related Scripture

Matthew 4:1-11
2 Corinthians 11:14
Ephesians 6:10-18
Hebrews 2:14-18; 4:14-16

Start time 16:11

Start cue
The singers sing, "'Young Herc' is mortal now."

End time 19:23

End cue
Hercules says, "I know it doesn't make any sense."

Clip summary

Hercules becomes a mortal man but keeps his supernatural strength. He goes into the village with his dad and creates such a stir that the entire marketplace is destroyed. The townspeople react in anger.

Materials

Cued video, TV, VCR, poster board, markers, Bible

Say

"Hercules was a very special man in Greek mythology. Samson was also a very special man in the Bible."

Ask students

◆ What was unique about Hercules?

Before the clip, say

"Let's watch a clip about Hercules. Then we will learn about another strong man."

 Show the video clip.

Ask students

◆ What did you learn about Hercules?
◆ What was special about him?

As the children mention facts about Hercules, make a list for the group. List Hercules' characteristics in one column along the left side of the poster board. Then you will write Samson's characteristics down the other side of the poster board.

Say

"Samson was also very strong. He was a real man who lived during Bible times."

Ask students

◆ What do you know about Samson?

Say

"Samson was strong like Hercules was. He did some pretty amazing things. He killed a lion with his bare hands. He pushed down a temple. He killed 1,000 Philistines with the jawbone of a donkey. Let's read about him and add to our list."

Read these Scripture references, then add Samson's characteristics to the list on the poster board: Judges 16:4-6, 17-30.

Ask students

◆ Why didn't Samson cut his hair?
◆ What happened when his hair was cut?
◆ Do you think Samson felt like he didn't fit in like Hercules did?

Say

"Samson's strength came from God, who God used in a powerful way. You may not have supernatural powers like Samson did, but God can use you too!"

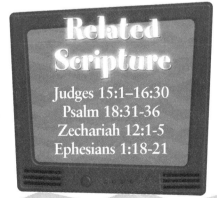

Related Scripture

Judges 15:1–16:30
Psalm 18:31-36
Zechariah 12:1-5
Ephesians 1:18-21

Start time 13:20

Start cue
Emily is getting out of the swimming pool.

End time 15:30

End cue
Cody says, "I think your reputation's safe."

Clip summary

Kids at the pool are making fun of Ryan for all kinds of reasons. He looks different. He's not from where they are. He fell into the swimming pool. He did a cannonball off of the high-dive platform.

Materials

Cued video, TV, VCR, marker board and marker or chalkboard and chalk

Say

"Kids can sometimes be really cruel. They make fun of other kids for all kinds of reasons."

Ask students

◆ Have you ever been teased? Why?
◆ Have you ever made fun of someone else?

Before the clip, say

"We are going to watch a video clip where a bunch of kids at a swimming pool are making fun of Ryan. Try to count all the ways they make fun of him."

 Show the video clip.

Ask students

◆ How many ways did the kids make fun of Ryan?
◆ What are all the ways the kids at the pool were cruel?

As students name ways the kids were cruel to Ryan, make a list on the board. Then, encourage students to add other ways that children can be mean by making fun of someone. Divide the children into groups of three or four. Have each group select one way in which children make fun of someone. First, let each group act out that cruel action, then have them act out an appropriate response to the situation. Have the groups perform for one another.

Ask students

◆ How does it feel when someone makes fun of you?
◆ How does it feel when you see someone being ridiculed?
◆ What can you do when you see someone being cruel?

Continue to rehearse ways to resist being bullied, ways to confront a bully, ways to derail bullying, and ways to stand up for someone who is being ridiculed.

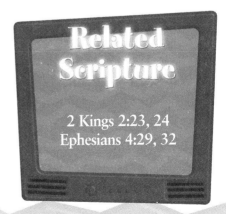

Related Scripture

2 Kings 2:23, 24
Ephesians 4:29, 32

Start time 2:78

Start cue
Mr. Vanderhill asks, "Walker, McCoy, can you hear me?"

End time 6:82

End cue
Josh's dad asks, "Is there something else you'd like to tell me? . . ."

Clip summary
Josh sees Simon break a drill bit in the shop at school. The shop teacher thinks Josh did it. Josh must decide whether to tell the truth and risk his dad's job or be punished for something he didn't do.

Materials
Cued video, TV, VCR, poster-board signs that read "tell the truth" and "cover up the truth"

Ask students
◆ Have you ever had a hard time telling the truth?
◆ Was it ever easier to lie than to tell the truth?
◆ Is it ever better to lie than to tell the truth?

Some children may answer yes. Guide them to see that lying is never better than telling the truth. There may be consequences for telling the truth but it is still better than lying. Telling the truth is always the right thing to do.

Before the clip, say

"We are going to watch part of a video where the main character Josh has to decide whether or not to tell the truth. Watch to see what would happen if Josh told the truth and what would happen if Josh lied."

 ## Show the video clip.

Ask students

◆ What would happen if Josh told the truth?
◆ Why is he afraid to tell the truth?
◆ What would happen if Josh continued to cover up the truth?
◆ Why do you think Josh is having trouble deciding what to do?

Have the children vote on what they think Josh should do. Tell them to vote "tell the truth" by standing on one side of the room and vote "cover up the truth" by standing on the other side of the room. This will force children to choose a side. When all the children have voted, discuss the two sides.

If Josh tells the truth, he puts his dad's job at risk. But telling the truth is the right thing to do. If Josh continues to cover up the truth, he will be punished, and his dad and teacher will be disappointed by his behavior.

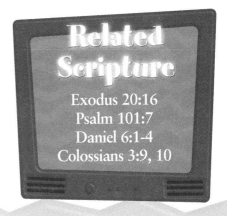

Related Scripture

Exodus 20:16
Psalm 101:7
Daniel 6:1-4
Colossians 3:9, 10

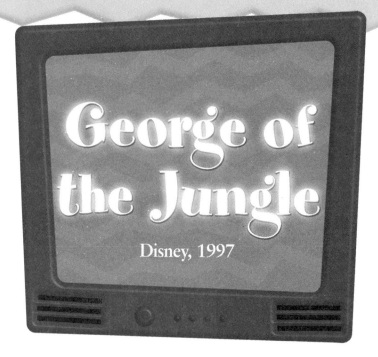

Start time 13:57

Start cue

Ursula says, "We can't go into the jungle alone. We could get lost out here."

End time 15:61

End cue

George says, "Bad kitty."

Clip summary

Ursula and Lyle encounter a lion—the king of the jungle. Lyle starts to run away, trips, and hits his head, knocking him out. George diverts the lion's attention away from Ursula just in time to save her.

Materials

Cued video, TV, VCR, Bible

Ask students

◆ Who is the king of the jungle?
◆ Why do you think the lion got the nickname "king of the jungle"?

Before the clip, say

"In the movie *George of the Jungle*, Ursula and her boyfriend Lyle come across a lion in the jungle. Let's watch to see what happens."

 Show the video clip.

Ask students

◆ What would be scary about meeting a lion in the jungle?
◆ Do you think someone like George would save you?

Say

"Someone is compared to a lion in the Bible. Let's read a few verses from the book of 1 Peter to see who it is."

Read 1 Peter 5:8, 9, which describes the devil as a lion looking for someone to devour.

Ask students

◆ In what ways is Satan like a lion?
◆ How could Satan devour someone like a lion would?

Say

"Satan is just waiting for the right opportunity to pounce on us. He wants us to trip and fall like Lyle did so that he can get us."

Ask students

◆ What happens when Satan pounces on us?
◆ What can we do when Satan pounces?

Lead students to see that this is what happens when we are tempted to sin. To resist temptation, sometimes we should run like Lyle did, even though we are afraid like Ursula was, and sometimes we have to stand up and fight like George did.

Ask students

◆ Do we have to fight Satan by ourselves? Why or why not?

Help the children understand that Jesus helps us when Satan tempts us. He will rescue us just as George rescued Ursula.

Related Scripture

Genesis 3:1-24
1 Corinthians 10:13
2 Corinthians 2:11
James 1:12-15; 4:1-10

Start time 23:32

Start cue

Madame Blueberry says, "Let's see, how does that song go?"

End time 23:79

End cue

The end of the song.

Clip summary

Madame Blueberry has learned the hard way that a thankful heart is a happy heart. She sings a song of thankfulness. The song emphasizes having an attitude of gratitude every day.

Materials

Cued video, TV, VCR, poster board, markers

Before the children arrive, print the following phrases on pieces of poster board: "Waking up," "Eating breakfast," "At school," "With friends at lunch," "Eating dinner with my family," "Going to bed."

 Show the video clip.

Ask students

◆ Madame Blueberry learned that a thankful heart is a happy heart. Do you agree with her?

◆ What are some reasons you can thank God every day?

Show the poster-board phrases you prepared earlier.

Say

"These are specific times in your typical day. We are going to brainstorm some things you can be thankful for at these particular times."

Have the children place each piece of poster board at a different spot in the room. Then walk as a group from station to station, discussing what you can be thankful for at those various times of the day.

Ask students

◆ What can you be thankful for in the morning when you wake up and begin your day?
◆ What can you be thankful for while you are at school?

Say

"Now we are going to pray, thanking God for some of these things we have mentioned."

Divide the children into groups of three. You may want to mix older and younger children or have an adult travel with the younger children, helping them focus their prayer thoughts.
   Each group will start at a different station, thanking God for appropriate things at that time of day, then proceed to another station. The groups will continue praying and moving to a new station until they have prayed at each station.

Related Scripture

Psalm 100
Luke 17:11-19
1 Thessalonians 5:18

Movie Index

Scripture Index